I am so excited to be able to bring these seemingly incongruous worlds together. Because caught between them both is this beautifully fragile moment of life – you, who deserves to be both wild and well heeled.

You are the universe, expressing itself as a human for a little while

Eckhart Tolle

*Y*ou weren't born in a suit, you probably never dreamed as a child of a job in corporate and in every objective, goal or target the one key element is you.

Corporates cannot exist without humans - they exist because of you.

This handbook is for you and about you. The you beyond the job title. The thinking, feeling bundle of love, pain, quirks, thoughts and feelings.

Because you will spend more of your lifetime within the workplace, this book has been designed to apply within this setting. We believe that if we can give you tools to implement changes here, then you will gain the most from them.

The Corporate Hippie condenses multiple schools of thought and knowledge into focused practices you can use in your day to day work that will become a habit that can resonate throughout every other aspect of your life.

Each chapter in the first section is focused on the human drivers behind most areas of issue we face within corporate. From. communication and fear through to self knowledge and love.

The second section goes into more depth into areas touched on in section one that you may be unfamiliar with, such as how to choose crystals, where to use aromatherapy, cartomancy and why moon cycles are useful.

Section one is enough to start creating real change in your life, Section 2 answers questions you may have about some of the practices and will perhaps lay the foundations for future study.

The objective of this book? To help you rebalance, to give you a different perspective, to enrich your time and enable you to harness the benefit of ancient knowledge within a modern workplace.

TABLE OF CONTENTS

WHY YOU, WHY NOW
HOW TO USE THIS BOOK

SECTION 1 - CORPORATE CHALLENGES

SELF KNOWLEDGE
FOUR FRIENDS
MIRROR, MIRROR ON THE WALL
GO WITH THEE FLOW...OF CONSCIOUSNESS
TIME LORDS
YOUR TOOL KIT

SUCCESS & OBSTACLES
SIGNS FOR SUCCESS
GET A THESAURUS
DREAM DRAWING
GET CLEANING
YOUR TOOLKIT

FEAR & WORRY
BURN BABY BURN
STORM IN A TEACUP
GET GROUNDED
THOUGHT COCOON BUTTERFLY
YOUR TOOLKIT

SUPPORT INTIMACY & LOVE
CRITICAL KARERN
HOW ARE YOU
DON'T TOUCH, FEEL
SENSATIONAL
YOUR TOOLKIT

PROTECTION
VISUALISE
WHAT GOES IN MUST COME OUT
YOUR CREATE YOUR REALITY
IF YOU CAN'T SWEEP IT - SHAKE IT OFF
YOUR TOOLKIT

PEACE OF MIND AND BALANCE
AS INTERNAL SO EXTERNAL
QUIETEN THE INTERNAL CHATTER
CONNECT WITH YOUR INTUITION
FROM 101 TO 3
YOUR TOOLKIT

COMMUNICATION
GET CLEAR ON THE OUTCOME
LEARN HOW TO LISTEN
ITS NEVER STUPID TO ASK
DON'T SPEAK
YOUR TOOLKIT

SECTION 2 - NEED TO KNOW

GROUNDING
CRYSTALS
DIVINATION TOOLS
CARTOMANCY
PENDULUMS
RUNES
YOUR SENSES
LISTEN TO THE RHYTHMS
THE MOON
RETROGRADES
THE PLANETS
THE SEASONS

ABOUT THE AUTHOR

WHY YOU, WHY NOW?

You are not just your job, you are far more. But with work gradually infringing upon not only our time but also our home space, it can be easy to lose that wild, free-spirited soul behind the never-ending emails, internal messages and video calls.

We see this in the way we introduce ourselves upon meeting new people - the most common response, even outside of the workplace is: "I am <insert job title>".

But you, that living, feeling, ball of individualism are not just your job.

By gently introducing practices seeped in nature and the spiritual world - whichever religion you practise, you can enjoy the buzz of working on a successful project, smashing the deadline and driving a career whilst also giving the human within yourself space to breathe.

To be both wild and well-heeled.

And there couldn't be a better time - corporate is changing. Although time is still money, stock-market analysts still expect Q on Q increases and competitors haven't stopped baying at the door. There is now far more respect for the individual behind the LinkedIn Profile.

Many companies are increasingly realising that you don't need to wear a three-piece suit to be taken seriously. That being sat at your desk until 2am working doesn't mean you are a hard worker. Above all that happy employees who have the space to bring their whole self to work - make innovative and dedicated employees.

By finding balance between business and the human you will find that you achieve better results, more meaningful work relationships and a happier you - full sleeve, pink hair, stripy socks and all.

Corporate is becoming more human, dare I say hippie – 24/7 anywhere, any device.

"WHAT YOU LEAVE BEHIND IS NOT WHAT IS ENGRAVED IN STONE MONUMENTS, BUT WHAT IS WOVEN INTO THE LIVES OF OTHERS

Pericles

HOW TO USE THIS BOOK

The Corporate Hippie Handbook has been created specifically for the time poor, overloaded professional to be able to maximise what time you have available to achieve impactful and lasting results that will resonate within you work life, home life and knowledge of yourself.

We have distilled a vast amount of information to give you targeted, focused tools and practices for specific situations. As such, The Corporate Hippie Handbook is Split into two sections - the first is full of targeted and actionable practices that you can navigate to as the need arises; the second section gives context and background knowledge into some of the elements that make up Section 1 and more which, you can flick through in your own time.

Section 1
The first section is divided into the individual roots or 'emotional drivers' that create emotional reactions. Here you will find succinct and simple practices, optimised for the office setting, that can help you gain balance within these areas. At the end of each section is a question to help you harness your minds eye. As your body does not know what is real or imagined - it just reacts to the emotion your mind creates, you can short-wire good memories to help your practices.

The Toolkits
The Toolkits can be found after each of the chapters in Section 1. See them as quite literally your place to go to for tools that will aid you in whatever emotional driver is at the helm of a situation. From crystals through to aromatherapy and sound - each sensory tool has been carefully selected for the impact they will have to aid you in whatever you are choosing to work on.

For questions about these tools, such as how to choose your crystals or the impact of sound on the body, or using the moon cycles, head over to Section 2. Here we will give context and background knowledge to an overview and foundational knowledge to each tool.

Section 2

The second part of the book is a mini overview clarifying some of the newer concepts such as divination, moon cycles and crystals. This section goes into more depth about some of the lesser known tools giving you a deeper knowledge that you can peruse in your own time to get the most out of your tools. It is full of foundation level insights upon which you can build upon if anything catches your imagination

www.corporatehippiehandbook.com

No book is complete without a website! Because we cover such a wide range of tools, which would have required multiple sites to source from we have put in the hard work for you and made these and more available from just one place.

Here you will also find additional materials, including actions plans for leaders and individuals as well as audio guides for the meditations

The information provided in this book is designed to provide helpful information on the subjects discussed. This book is not meant to be used, nor should it be used, to diagnose or treat any medical condition. For diagnosis or treatment of any medical problem, consult your own physician.

Your Challenges

SECTION ONE

This Section covers the main challenges you will face. Because the majority of the challenging situations can be boiled down to 7 main areas, or roots we have condensed them down to:

- Self Knowledge
- Success & Obstacles
- Fear & Worry
- Support, Intimacy & Love
- Protection
- Peace of Mind and Balance
- Communication

Over the next few pages you will find succinct and simple practices, optimised for the office setting, that can help you gain balance within each these areas.

These practices have been chosen both their simplicity and also their impact. You do not need to have any background in meditation, or spend extensive time practicing them to get results. Although, as with everything in life, the more frequently you engage them the more insights arise and long term benefits will arise.

Because this book is intended to work with you, not prescribe, we have left space for notes after each section introduction for you to consider your perceptions of them and what they mean for you.

Taking time to formulate your thoughts in ways you perhaps have not previously considered will help you to understand yourself on a deeper level and enable you to access insights you perhaps hadn't realised were within you all along.

Self Knowledge

KNOWING YOURSELF IS THE BEGINING OF ALL WISDOM

Aristotle

SELF KNOWLEDGE

We are not fixed marks. We are ever-changing, ever-moving balls of energy. And in today's society we are doing this at an ever-increasing rate as the people, experiences and situations we can come across, increase.

The relationship you need with yourself to have Self-Knowledge is similar to the one you have with a dear friend. When you first meet someone, you get to know them by talking to them, listening to what they say and how they say it. If a friendship develops, you will probably catch up with them on what's new, how they are feeling, their highs and lows. In other words you stay up-to-date with their life, how they are changing and who they are becoming.

How often do we give this time to ourselves? To take a moment to sit down and just reflect on how we feel, keep in touch on how we are changing? Life quite literally runs away with us. We become lost in the to-dos, will-dos, omg-I-completely-forgots, and I-should-haves. Today we live loud and we live fast. And in this, the one very important thing that tends to gets left behind is you.

Often changes are imperceivable; they can happen so gradually that we don't notice them until life throws us a curveball and we realise our world doesn't quite align with who we are anymore. Then it can be hard to listen and sometimes even harder to accept what you discover when you do begin to realign.

Over the next chapter you will find practices that you can implement today to reconnect and stay connected. Every journey you embark on in life that starts from a place of self knowledge, will begin in the right direction.

Practice 1 - Four Friends

One of the best exercises I have come across for increasing self-knowledge was while I was training in the old ways as an Awenydd. It will take you completely back to the basic parts of what makes you who you are – your thoughts, emotions, body and intuition. Think of these as the foundations, cornerstones or compass points of what makes you...you. Connecting with them regularly will not only help you feel more balanced and become a guidance but also bring you back to the essence of you - beyond social constructs, belief systems and your environment.

As with most of the practices in this handbook *try to* Listen without expectation, accept what you find without judgement and remember that when we communicate on deeper levels, how we receive information is not always straight forward.

Step 1: Divide a piece of paper into four parts an at the top of each part write Thinking, Emotion, Body, Intuition

Step 2: Find a quiet place and sit comfortably. Close your eyes, focus on your breath, let your mind and body release and find your centre. (There isn't a map or a prescribed feeling to identify your individual centre – just focus on where you want to be – trust yourself and you will know when you arrive there.)

Step 3: Spend some time in your centre and stay there until you feel ready to continue.

Step 4: You now want to take yourself to connect with Thinking. Imagine yourself moving into a room where you can connect with Thinking.

Step 5: Out loud or silently greet Thinking like you would an old friend you hadn't seen for many years - you might feel the need to apologise for not having visited them or spent time with them. Ask Thinking, "What do you feel about my life right now? Do you have any guidance, advice or information for me?

Step 6: Now be still and listen – be aware of thoughts, images, sensations, feelings, colours and smells that come to you.

Step 7: When you're ready, thank Thinking for their time and guidance, take yourself back to your centre and draw, write or scribble what came to you during that session then return to centre.

Step 8: Repeat with Emotions, Body and Intuition, each time returning to the centre and jotting down what came to you.

Step 9: Once you return to the centre for the last time, stay there a while and let yourself feel the experience. You might find other images or sensations arise – listen to them.

When you feel it's time, open your eyes, go make yourself a good cup of coffee and reflect on what messages you received.

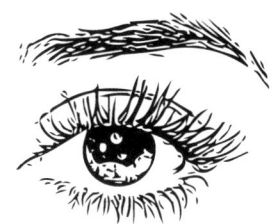

Practice 2: Mirror, Mirror on the Wall

When was the last time you looked at yourself - I mean really looked?

You know that feeling when you stare into someone's eyes and all of a sudden, the world implodes around you into that moment as you realise maybe there is a doorway to the soul.

Step 1: Find a mirror or use the camera on your phone - stand it up so you can clearly see your face in it.

Step 2: Look, really look into that person's eyes. What shape are the eyes? Which colours can you see in the pupils? What patterns can you make out in the flecks? How large are the irises? How does one differ from the other?

Step 3: Lay out a piece of paper and pick up a pencil. Now with the same attention to detail, you just gave your eyes, draw your face - everything that you can see. Don't pay attention to the aesthetic quality of what you draw; just pay attention to you.

Step 4: When you have finished, spend some time with what you have drawn and notice the emotions or feelings it brings up. This image is a great place to start to look at how you view yourself.

Step 5: Finish the practice by looking at your self-portrait with compassion, love, and thanks. Without that person in front of you - you wouldn't be where you are today.

SELF KNOWLEDGE

Practice 3: Go with the Flow...of Consciousness

The hustle and bustle of the day-to-day can crowd our heads so that there is barely time to think about what to cook for dinner, let alone even consider delving into ourselves.

Writers often use the practice below to help them with the creative block - it also functions incredibly well as a tool to bypass the mind's restrictive chatter and get into your stream of consciousness. In this stream you will find a wealth of insights that will give you an accurate pulse on where you are right now as well as keys to what you need most at this moment in time.

Step 1: Grab a pen, and a blank sheet of paper then set a timer on your phone for 3 minutes

Step 2: Imagine you are introducing yourself to a new acquaintance. Write on the paper "Hi, my name is <insert name>, and I am..."

Step 3: Now, without removing your pen from the paper, continue writing until your alarm goes off. Don't worry about what you are writing, just let your pen continue to mark words upon the page - let them flow, unfettered and uncensored.

Step 4: Read through what you have written how does that resonate with you? What has come up you weren't expecting? Are there any actions you want to take?

Note: You can play around with the initial sentence depending on what you need at a specific moment in time - for example, you could start with "Today I am...." or "This week I need..."

Practice 4: Time Lords

Ever-increasingly we look to external sources for answers. We have become out of the practice of asking ourselves, even worse - we no longer trust the answers we arrive at if we do ask. You may or may not be surprised to hear that what many mystery schools teach is founded on innate power within yourself and how to harness it.

The below is an adaption of exercises taught to help you develop your intuition, which, with practice, will also function to help you to re-learn to trust your inner knowledge..

Step 1: Without looking at a clock, watch, or phone ask yourself what time it is. Don't try to 'guess' and base the time on the position of the sun, how hungry you feel or when your last meeting was. Let the first numbers that come up in your mind that bubble up bypassing active thought and use these.

Step 2: Check the time. If you get it right, recall the difference between using your thought and using your intuition. Remember it for next time.

You may or may not get it right straight away. Like most people don't suddenly run a marathon without any training - practice is key. Keep at it, and you will soon surpass the initial surprise when you begin to grow increasingly accurate and from there start to develop both trust and deep respect for your inner knowledge.

Adaption: You can try this practice across various mediums - with letters before you open them; emails before you open up your inbox or phone calls before you look at the screen. **SELF KNOWLEDGE**

Your Toolkit

Top Essential Oils to Help Enhance Self-Knowledge

Lemongrass promotes a feeling of being centred and aids in clearing the mind, letting go of the old and making space for the new

Geranium helps the mind to focus and promotes balanced male and female energies

Myrrh cultivates wisdom and self-healing

Crystals

Labradorite encourages self-awareness of intuition; it will enhance your awareness and self-discovery. Use it to find the answers to questions you didn't even realise you had.

Moonstone will gently guide self-discovery, enabling true and honest communication with yourself without judgement

Feldspar is a stone of creativity and problem solving however it is also powerful for self-awareness assisting in the discovery of previously overlooked messages

Listen

Sound is incredibly powerful, if you have never been to a Gong meditation, then find one near you, pack a mat some blankets a pillow and enjoy. Gong meditation is an immersive experience of sound and its vibrations. Lead by an experienced practitioner, it will allow you to relax and go deep within yourself completely.

If there isn't anywhere close by, or your short on time then head over to www.corporatehippiehandbook.com and we have links to some fantastic Gong Meditations you can click on and start immediately.

Using Colour to Aid Self Knowledge

Self Knowledge is all about reflection. Deep hues such as dark blues and greens will help to calm the mind and create space for this. You can find colour anywhere - from an item of clothing to sourcing a specific notebook cover (you could even go old school and hand-cover your favourite notebook with a deep blue or green paper!).

If your really stuck pull up a powerpoint presentation, stick a deep blue square in the middle and gaze at that for a moment or two.

SELF KNOWLEDGE

Your notes:

Your notes:

SELF KNOWLEDGE

Success & Obstacles

> THE SECRET OF CHANGE IS TO FOCUS ALL OF YOUR ENERGY, NOT ON FIGHTING THE OLD, BUT ON BUILDING THE NEW

Socrates

SUCCESS & OBSTACLES

Success is all about growth. Our focus of energy towards success drives us towards, not just the object we aim for, but it also the road we will follow beyond that once attained.

Your energy and the time spent using it is precious - make sure you spend it well.

Every time we aim our arrow towards a target, whether we set it ourselves or otherwise, we develop. However, it's not actually hitting the target that develops us. Instead, it is each time that we aim and miss it that enables our growth. It is only on missing that we learn to readapt our stance, poise or tension on the bow so that we become capable of achieving what we set out to do.

Success can be tangible such as getting a promotion or intangible such as feeling confidence whilst presenting at an annual meeting. It can be something you judge personally or something that someone else judges for you.

Whatever your success is and whoever it is judged by, one thing is certain - just as a hero is a hero by achieving something beyond the average, success is success because we arrive there only by overcoming a difficulty or difficulties. Becoming what we need to be to achieve what we set our mark on.

'These 'difficulties' don't need to be painful - we can make the journey towards success one of self-discovery, interest and learning that has positive ramifications throughout all aspects of our life.

Practice 1: Signs for Success

When working on a goal, feelings of inadequacy or inability, sometimes even unworthiness can consume us. Transforming our goals from language processed in the logical right brain into symbols allows us to give them a life of their own beyond the logic of the present and its perceived limitations.

Step 1: Write down your intention or goal on a piece of paper. As you do it, feel what achieving this goal will be like:

I will be promoted next quarter

Step 2: Now remove all of the repeating vowels and consonants –

I W L B E P R O M T D N X Q U A

Step 3: Make a pattern or picture with these letters, they can be any angle, size and can overlap – have fun with it, put passion into it and while you do, imagine how you will feel achieving it.

If you can't make head or tail of your original sentence in the symbol that is perfect! The purpose of this exercise is to make the symbol unidentifiable – we are working to manifest your intentions directly to your subconscious. In doing so, we bypass the logic and murky waters of the consciousness where lack of self-belief or feelings of unworthiness can cause self-sabotage.

Step 4: Once you have fitted in all of the letters in the picture etch the symbol onto a white candle, sit in a quiet place, light it and let it burn down.

Supercharge your practices by aligning them with the Luna calendar. For all new ventures, including new challenges and goals, start them under the new moon or waxing moon. The waxing energy will boost your practice.

Practice 2 – Get a Thesaurus

What you hear influences your perception and as such, how you interact with it. Choosing our words wisely will help positively influence our perspective on challenges. Whilst many words can be used interchangeably, they are not all made equal!

Step 1: Close your eyes for a moment and envisage the word 'obstacle' obstacle - what images, thoughts or feelings come up for you?

Step 2: Repeat step one with the word 'Challenge'.

Step 3: Consider which you would prefer to find upon your path towards success.

Step 4: Consider other words you use that could be swapped out for a more inspirational words

Get yourself a thesaurus, check out some synonyms and get to grips with the subtleties in each word to start turning obstacles into welcome challenges, study into expanding your skillset, and deficits into development opportunities. Take not of how the change of word impacts your perspective on what you are facing.

It will be worth its weight in aurous, or should I say gold!

Practice 3 – Dream Drawing

The practice of vision boards is still in circulation for a reason - it works. Vision boards do two things – they move the goal from your mind into physical space, and secondly, the visual reminder serves as motivation if or rather when, the going gets tough.

Drawing what is in your mind over finding an image already created is a far more effective way of building your vision board. It is quite literally taking what is in your head and giving it a physical form.

Step 1: Sit quietly and imagine achieving success in your goal. Ask yourself - How will it feel? What images or colours best represent that feeling? What will that success bring you - a new car, holidays, a dog or ability to communicate in a different language? What images, colour or words best represent your success in your mind's eye?

Step 2: Take what is in your mind's eye and give it a form in reality - sketching, colouring everything that embodies your success onto a piece of paper (leftover cereal box makes for an awesome board FYI!)

Step 3: Stick, tape, pin this somewhere where your eye will catch it daily and every time it does – recreate that feeling of having achieved the success. Really imagine yourself driving that car, the look on the faces of those you are speaking to in that new language, what you will be doing under that sunshine in Hawaii – really every bit of it.

Supercharge your practices by aligning them with the Luna calendar. For all new ventures, including new challenges and goals, start them under the new moon or waxing moon. The waxing energy will boost your practice.

SUCCESS & OBSTACLES

Practice 4 – Get Cleaning

Ever notice that whenever there is a problem in your life - you are always present? The practice of Ho-oponopono looks at how you are responsible for everything you think, for everything that comes to your attention - the amazing, the good, the bad and the dam right ugly.

So, whatever is in your reality now that doesn't make you feel good - be it person, news, emotion, or situation - roll your sleeves up, get cleaning!

Step 1: Love it - yes, whatever it is, I feel it with all your heart. Send love, enwrap the feeling, challenge or person in love. Then let that love trickle over into everything in your life, you, your body, your work, your house.

Step 2: Say sorry to that emotion, situation or person. Whatever it is - just step beyond that wall of ego and say it, "I am sorry", "I am sorry", "I am sorry", "I am sorry"...

Step 3: Ask for forgiveness - it doesn't matter who or what - just let yourself get humble and ask for it. Your not admitting guilt, your just giving forgiveness.

Step 4: Show gratitude - say thank you. Thank it for coming into your awareness, thank it for accepting your forgiveness, thank yourself for allowing forgiveness, thank the universe, the world, the ground you walk upon. Say "Thank you" until you feel everything around you glowing a little brighter

Step 5: How do you feel now?

WHAT WAS YOUR LAST SUCCESS? HOW DID IT FEEL?

Use Biographical Visualisation to reconnect with a past memory and manifest the sensations again within your present. By doing this you are reaffirming your ability to feel them and reinforcing the pathways to receive them again.

SUCCESS & OBSTACLES

Your Toolkit

Top Essential Oils to Help Enhance Success & Overcoming Obstacles

Rosemary stimulates the mind, promotes concentration, boosts self esteem and mental clarity

Orange bright and energising this will encourage adaptability

Jasmine releases mental blocks, strengths confidence, associated with good luck

Clary Sage energising and rejuvenating, increases flow of inspiration and supports decision making

Crystals

Roll around a piece of Labourite in your palm – and sit quietly with it for a while. This gemstone, renown for its ability to connect to higher wisdom and your subconscious mind, is linked to your third eye and crown chakra. It will help you dig deep within yourself and find solutions where you didn't realise they could exist.

Listen

Time to stick in those earphones, close your eyes and clear your mind for as long as you feel necessary. What you listen to is going to stimulate your brain into problem-solving space, so that when you turn your mind to the problem at hand, your brain is warmed up. Binaural beats with lower beta frequencies between 14 to 30Hz are linked to increased alertness, problem-solving ability and concentration.

Colour

Colours that have the greatest wavelength and require more energy to understand, stimulate the brain, so think red, orange, yellows. If the sunset doesn't appear when you need it or your stuck in a meeting just pop on your phone and search for it. instead. It is definitely not as good as the real thing, but the colours will be on point!

Touch

Massage those earlobes and wake up multiple energy points in your body, stimulating the pituitary and pineal glands in your brain to create a feeling of relaxation and burst of energy!

SUCCESS & OBSTACLES

Your notes:

Your notes:

SUCCESS & OBSTACLES

Overcoming Fear & Worry

FEAR IS THE BOUNDARY THAT LIES BETWEEN US AND A WORLD OF POSSIBILITIES

OVERCOMING FEAR & WORRY

Shambhala, teaches that we cling on to fears because they protects us. We live with fear to the extent that we can quite comfortably co-exist with it in our daily lives without even realising.

Our fear is anything outside the known or predictable. Over the years, through experience, we build up what is essentially our 'safe zone'. Habits, friendships, mindset, thoughts that are familiar keep us protected and become, with the years, the stones that build walls around us.

Within these walls we feel safe, but we are also restricted.

Fear makes us build fortresses and then willingly enclose ourselves inside, locked within ways of thinking and being. We are safe, but we are not living fully. We are trapped, in stasis and stuck.

We all have fears, and we always will – it's how our minds function to protect us. We are alive today because our ancestors, when chilling on the savanna, ran when they saw a rustle in the grass without waiting to find out if it was dangerous or not. Our minds are our greatest assets, they are also our greatest enemy. Just as they create the dreams we aim for they also just as creatively construct the nightmares from which we hide.

Nowadays you're unlikely to be in a life or death situation, let's face it – a big presentation to the boss, a meeting request from HR after a difficult financial quarter or finding a mistake in an important document isn't going to kill you. But your body doesn't know that and your mind, from behind those fortress walls isn't comfortable being forced outside them.

So how can we learn to let some sunlight through those walls, and face situations which make us fear fearful with more peace?

Practice 1 - Burn Baby Burn

With the hindsight of many years and sometimes a few grey hairs we can look back and recognise fears, see the place they had in our lives, and why. But when we are in the moment, we often find it difficult to consciously step outside of the emotions to recognise the fears that may be driving them.

Do this practice in conjunction with a specific situation that you are feeling intense emotions about or for general overview to draw out what may be lurking in the shadows.

Step 1: Take a pen and paper and write down what scares you. It might be work-related or not - love, money, security, skills - get it all out on that white page.

Step 2: Read through each fear on your list and repeat after each one "I release you."

Step 3: With a candle or lighter put flame to your list, watching as the paper and your fears flicker in the light, becoming smaller and smaller.

Step 4: Throw the ashes in a westward direction to set with the sun.

To supercharge this practice, perform it during a waning moon, which will help to drain out their energy even further to kick-off to the next new moon with a positive start.

Practice 2 - Making Storms in Teacups

Failure is one of those words that almost comes with its own personal silence after it. For many of us, it is synonymous with those primary school test papers covered with red pen marks – nothing ever good seemed to come from getting a bad grade, grazed knees, or a battered ego. Well, good did come from it – it meant we tried harder, we learnt the lessons, and sometimes we even mastered them.

The exercise below will help you push fear into the box of perspective. You will be playing fear at its own game, that of unnecessary exaggeration. This practice will bring all the emotion-inducing elements involved in fear or worry from the shadow and into the logical light of day.

Ready to create a storm in a teacup?

Step 1: On the centre of a piece of paper, write down what worries you.

Step 2: Around it brainstorm all the things that could happen if your fear or worry came to fruition - the worse possible cases e.g.
- Don't hit sales target
- Miss bonus
- I lose my job
- Cant pay the mortgage or bills
- Declare bankruptcy and become homeless

Step 3: Take now work on each of those points you have just brainstormed and engage your creative, problem-solving prowess.
- You miss your bonus - what do you need to do to hit the next one?
- You become homeless, who could you stay with?
- You can't pay the bills - where else could you earn money?

The likelihood is that when all the chips are down, you would still be able to find a roof over your head, get food in your tummy and have your health. These are the only things you need for any great new venture.

Practice 3 - Get Grounded

Our body is a part of everything else around us; it is nature within itself. Nature is deeply calm, stable and rhythmic. Connecting to earth is like plugging yourself into recharge.

When the adrenaline rush induced by fear or worry hits your body, connecting to nature will help you rebalance, gain perspective and real back some control.

Step 1: Get outside – whether it is in your back garden or a park

Step 2: Take your shoes off, stretch those toes and dig them into the earth, really grasp that connection

Step 3: Walk if you feel like walking, or if you prefer just stay standing in your space

Step 4: Imagine roots extending from your feet deep into the earth

Step 5: Focus on breathing. With every inhale, visualise the energy from the earth absorbing through the soles of your feet

Step 6: With every exhale, visualise your energy flowing down into the earth

Step 7: When you are ready on an inward breath thank the earth and draw your roots up back in through your soles

Practice 4 - Thought Cocoon Butterfly

Silence is uncomfortable for the majority of us. Especially if it is within our own head. You will have probably found that your mind has a barrage of thoughts that seem to spring into action the moment you try to meditate, or find some silence inside.

The thoughts that our mind throws up form part of what is known in Shambhala as our cocoon - what we surround ourselves with to 'protect' us from discomfort. We are so used to our cocoon, those patterns of behaviour and thoughts, that we are hardly aware of it. This practice will help you identify what thoughts your cocoon consists of and at the same time, start to get comfortable being outside of your cocoon.

Step 1: Sit comfortably in a position on the floor or a seat, with both feet flat on the ground

Step 2: Set your gaze to the ground about 5 meters away from your body and focus on your breath. Allow thoughts to come if they come, acknowledge them, then let them pass

Step 4: When your ready move your gaze to a meter away from your body and maintain it there, acknowledging the thoughts that come letting them pass. Recognise the different intensity you feel as your eyes draw closer to where you sit.

Step 5: Return your gaze to 5meters away and notice the difference this makes to your feelings and thoughts.

You will have found it more challenging to spend time with your gaze closer to your body - the thoughts become louder, you may feel irritated, tired - anything to distract you from the silence.

Make note of the thoughts that came into your mind during the practice. They will help you understand more about what you protect yourself with and enable you, should you wish, to look consider why you use them and whether they still serve you.

WHAT WAS A FEAR OR WORRY YOU HAVE OVERCOME?

Use Biographical Visualisation to reconnect with a past memory and manifest the sensations again within your present. By doing this you are reaffirming your ability to feel them and reinforcing the pathways to receive them again.

OVERCOMING FEAR & WORRY

Your Toolkit

Top Essential Oils to Help with Fear and Worry

Fennel is fantastic to relieve anxiety and stress to induce feelings of tranquillity. When used with Bergamot and Lavender oils, it can also enhance mental clarity. Great for when your inner chimp begins to blur your logic.

Frankincense not only smells beautiful but is super powerful in removing negativity from the environment, the body, aura and psyche. Frankincense also relaxes the diaphragm and as such encourages deeper breathing to help combat the shallower breath that the stress fear and worry can cause.

Top Crystals

Stick some hematite tumble stones in your pocket – these are incredibly grounding helping keep you closer to the earth's natural frequencies - when you're grounded, you are going to feel more relaxed and balanced. These little oil coloured crystals will help eliminate stress and anxiety from the body.

Aquamarine, from the same family as emerald, is found in granite rocks. Known as 'water of the sea' it will calm your mind and help to cleanse it of negative thoughts.

Listen

Engage your root chakra by listening to the 396 Hz Solfeggio Frequency - associated with the primary energy centre. Listening will help you ground those wild emotions and help release the nervous energy created by worry and fear.

Colour

Think cool calm light colours. Especially those found in nature. If you can't get outside though, your ability to access memories or create images will serve you just as well. Just as your body reacts to your fear and worry as a real life threatening danger whether it s a lion in-front of you or a hard to hit deadline, your body will also react to images your brain processes or remembers of calm places, beautiful skies or cool waters. So close your eyes and start remembering.

Touch

Mudras are hand gestures that can tap into the perpetual blissful state within us all. The Vayu Mudra specifically helps to connect with the earth, it will assist in reducing fatigue, keeping grounded and releasing irrational thoughts.

To do the Vayu Mudra, touch the tip of your thumb with the tip of your ring finger, keeping the other fingers extended.

It is not recommended to do this Mudra lying down

OVERCOMING FEAR & WORRY

Your notes:

Your notes:

**OVERCOMING FEAR
& WORRY**

Support, Intimacy & Love

WHAT YOU THINK YOU BECOME
WHAT YOU FEEL YOU ATTRACT
WHAT YOU IMAGINE YOU CREATE

Budda

SUPPORT, INTIMACY & LOVE

Support, Intimacy and Love - elements we all search for when we feel their lack in our lives. The only problem is that when we go in search of them, it usually is externally focused and often involving an 'other'. Rarely do we turn our gaze inward.

When we look for this support, it's often from someone we know who has a sympathetic voice or who has a shoulder to lean on. Because chances are you like most humans are a harsh critic of yourself. That little but persistent internal voice wouldn't dream of talking to another person the way it speaks to you.

What if you started to speak to yourself with more respect and compassion, to give yourself more support and love?

Think about yourself as a bare patch of earth – you must cultivate the ground, then sow seeds and only after this will a garden start to grow and attract pollinators. There are positive aftereffects when you focus your energy on fertilising your soul, becoming more intimate with yourself and the fabric of the world around you. You will not only fall in love with your world, your body and the mind that processes its sensations but also attract the same into your life.

Practice 1 - Critical Karen

Step 1: Over a few days listen to your inner voice and how you talk to yourself – you don't need to do anything other than start to be conscious of the way you treat yourself.

Step 2: Write down in a list all the ways you criticise yourself, how what you are doing is not enough; how you might not be enough.

Step 3: Imagine you're talking to a dear friend. Take each item on your list, write the positives for each or ways to work on and improve each. Opposite this list – note all the things you have done.

For example:

I take too long to do things	What I produce is accurate and thought through
I have no idea what I am talking about half of the time	My advice is accepted and actioned by your peers with success

Step 4: Rip the list down the middle with the negatives on one side and the positives on the other.

Step 5: Take the negative list and (in a safe place) put a match to the paper and release those words. To supercharge this, do it during the waning moon.

Step 6: Pin the list somewhere you can see it for a week – every day, repeat the positive sentences. After the end of the week, bury your list under a tree, let it nourish the roots, and watch your words grow.

To supercharge this during a waxing moon or in the days around a full moon.

Practice 2 – How are You?

We all want people to care for us, to ask us how we are, and to be able to respond with an open heart. We need to make room in our lives to allow support, intimacy, and love to enter in.

Step 1: Start by opening up space to allow others to become intimate with your vulnerability. Some may not be compassionate, but there are many more who will welcome the opportunity to assist where they may not have realised you needed it. You will find the more you open up – others will open up with you

Step 2: When people ask 'how are you' don't intuitively respond. You know that conversation as you fly past someone:

"How are you?"
"Great thanks, and you?"
"Yeah, great thanks."

Start responding to this question truthfully. Give time to each interaction and person who asks such an intimate question. It's not negativity if things aren't great for you that morning – its honesty. No one is going to be great every day, and everyone else around you knows it because they are human too.

Step 3: Stay present in these conversations, and you will find that people will start opening up to you, allowing you to enter their intimate life and vice-versa.

Practice 3 – Don't Touch - Feel

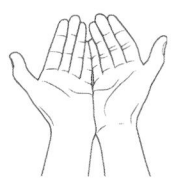

When all the chips are down - we are only really a collection of atoms vibrating together surrounded by other clusters of atoms vibrating at a different frequency. An ancient practice in many cultures is the laying of hands to pass energy through our palms to heal. Our hands are incredibly sensitive, but we so often use them more for their practical uses than their sensory ones. With this exercise, you will rebalance this.

Step 1: Find a quiet place where you can lie down or sit undisturbed, close your eyes, and rub your palms together.

Step 2: Breath in and out. Emphasise on your outward breath. Imagine the air flowing down your arms and out through your palms like a white, energising light.

Step 3: Place your palms facing your body and either place then on the body or allow them to hover from a few cms distance.

Step 4: Starting from the top of your head, allow your palms to slowly move around your head, over your ears, eyes, mouth and down the neck. Pause on your shoulders then slowly move your palms down each arm in turn, then over your torso. Adapt your position so you can reach your legs and repeat on each leg until you get to your toes. Throughout this practice, feel your outward breath moving through your palms.

Adaption
Instead of imagining your palms as giving energy, use them as sensors. As you move around our body keep your consciousness in your palms, feel the subtleties of energy, changes in warmth heat, pulsing. Make a note where you feel more 'activity', and either focus entirely or just for more extended periods in these areas when you practice the above.

SUPPORT, INTIMACY & LOVE

Practice 4 – Turn your Eyes on and Taste that Sound

Intimacy with another is that feeling of being close physically and/or emotionally with another. It is the result of a focus of attention that brings about feelings of connection. Unfortunately, nowadays our attention is frequently divided between multiple screens, devices, and to-dos. We rarely make time to give the intimacy we so crave - not just with each other but with our very foundations - the world around us.

We do not just exist on the earth; we are a part of her only and vice-versa. So strip off everything that stands between you and your experience of your world by getting intimate through your senses.

Pick one of these 5 senses to focus on each day:

- Taste
    - when you eat, turn off all distractions and focus on the taste of your food
- Sight
    - whenever you walk into a room imagine turning your eyes 'on' and becoming wider - make a point of noticing as much as you can
- Sound
    - close your eyes and make a mental note of each noise,
    - try and figure out what is causing the sound and where it is coming from as precisely as possible
- Touch
    - hold your hands out in front of you, now roll each fingertip against the tip of your thumb one by one, consider how each finger creates a different sensation for you
    - whenever your skin comes into contact with a surface or material, pause to recognise how it feels

WHEN DID YOU LAST FEEL AT PEACE?

Use Biographical Visualisation to reconnect with a past memory and manifest the sensations again within your present. By doing this you are reaffirming your ability to feel them and reinforcing the pathways to receive them again.

SUPPORT, INTIMACY & LOVE

Your Toolkit

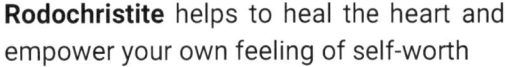

Top Essential Oils to Help with Support, Intimacy and Love

Essential oils, incense, or candles with lavender, jasmine, cypress, peppermint, tea tree and eucalyptus will tap into the sense of self and work to open your throat and heart chakras.

If you don't have any oils to hand, improvise and try a peppermint tea. If your at home plant jasmine in your garden and wander outside around dusk - the perfume will make your heart sing.

Top 6 Crystals

These crystals worn over your heart chakra, or in a breast pocket will have a wonderful impact. If Jewellery isn't your thing and you tend to lose tumble stones, have a search for coasters or keyrings with these stones.

Rodochristite helps to heal the heart and empower your own feeling of self-worth

Rhondonite assists to open our hearts to give and receive love, especially for those who have opened their hearts and were wronged in the past

Rose quartz the stone of universal love, purifies and opens up the heart to promote self-love and friendship

Malecite helps to get rid of negative belief systems that are holding you back

Listen

Thought to connect our heart, spiritual nature, and the divine harmony is the 528 Hz Solfeggio Frequency aka the love frequency. So pop onto youtube, get those headphones on and enjoy.

Colour

Traditionally the colours of love and intimacy are pinks and red. As such many of the crystals which assist in support, intimacy and love are these colours.

But when it comes to the self, the closest colour is the one you will find behind closed eyelids. The soft dark depths of you and only you lie behind them. Close your eyelids and allow yourself to rest within whatever you find there. Its uniquely your space that no-one else can enter, see or ever experience except you.

Touch

Our hands give so much to others, from handshakes that show our warmth through to the ability to massage, stroke and caress. What we can give we can also receive.

Turn your palms to direct that same love and compassion they so often show to others. Rub your palms together to get those 17,000 touch receptors and free nerve endings in the palm working for you. Then place them on your upper trapezius muscles in-between your neck and shoulders. Use your fingertips to rub them. You will feel enveloped in a giant ball of warmth and love in no time.

SUPPORT, INTIMACY & LOVE

Your notes:

Your notes:

SUPPORT, INTIMACY & LOVE

Protection

PROTECTION

We all it some point will enter situations in which we feel vulnerable or worse still, threatened.

The body will try to protect you, when you begin to feel this happening often so instinctively you won't even realise. From speeding up your heart beat to get the blood pumping in case you need to run, through to folded arms and slumped shoulders as it tries to make you as small a target as possible.

Perceived or real threats from many different places — individuals, situations and even yourself. Some may be driven by malicious intent, others in a completely unassuming context.

Before starting this chapter, it's important to consider your boundaries and how your communicate them — what are you okay with and what are you not okay with? What us acceptable to you and what isn't? Set your boundaries where they feel right for you - it doesn't matter what others do or seem to feel.

Once you have done this, whenever you feel they are being crossed, open a space for you and whatever or whoever is making you feel vulnerable (this includes yourself, if you are the cause) and discuss.. The more you do this, you will begin to trust yourself, to feel that you are in control and make positive changes in difficult situations when they arise.

What follows are a some great practices that you can implement today to start feeling more protected.

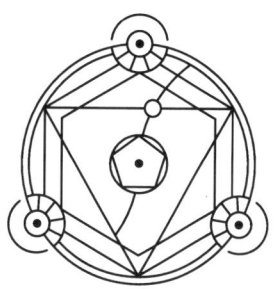

Practice 1 - Visualise

Protection comes from the Latin word, *'protegere'* meaning to cover with something. The images we consider for 'protection' in the modern-day range from security locks to armed guards which are going to be slight overkill in a corporate environment! So we will look at what you can do without anything else - just you, yourself and your mind's eye.

Step 1: Close your eyes and draw your focus to your energy (how you feel it will feel different for everyone - you might feel tingling, warmth or light among others)

Step 2: In your mind's eye draw another circle of energy around yourself and feel it protecting you from all external negative energy

Adaption: If you prefer, imagine opening an umbrella between yourself and the other person or situation,. Imagine it catching any unwanted energy before it hits you

Note: This visualisation works both ways - as you grow more conscious of how others impact you – you will also grow more aware of how you affect others. No-one is a full-time shining beacon of virtue and happiness; we have all got up on the wrong side of the bed – so it's important to learn how to protect others from your energy as well. To do this just imagine the circle of light around the other, or the umbrella between them open towards you, protecting them.

Practice 2 – What Goes in Must Come Out

When in situations where we feel threatened, it is all too easy for our chimp brain to jump into action, send a rush of adrenaline throughout your body, increasing your heart rate and your breathing. To help reverse this, we can start by taking back control of our breath.

Step 1: Before entering a difficult situation, take a few moments to focus on breathing - in through your nose for four seconds and out through your mouth for eight seconds. You can do this anywhere – walking to the meeting room, whilst getting a coffee or sat waiting for colleagues to join.

Step 2: When inside the situation, keep drawing your focus back to your breath. This will not only calm you but also make you feel more in control.

Remember that with every breath you are directing an element of nature – air, which also happens to be your life force. Nothing anyone can throw at you is more powerful than this.

You are powerful.

Practice 3 - You Create Your Reality

If you expect negativity you are going to find it somewhere - the tone of voice, facial expressions or words – whether the intention behind them was negative or not.

Always remember to check in with yourself and your expectations - if you are expecting a difficult situation that will impact how you receive information. Something said harmlessly could be taken as negative if we have entered that conversation dubious about our interlocutor's intentions.

Step 1: Enter every situation expecting to find love, compassion and happiness.

Step 2: Every time you feel like something is intentioned the wrong way – imagine it was said with love or by someone you know has good intentions for you.

If you want to see the impact of your expectations - go for a walk for 5 minutes and imagine that you are someone no-one wants to be around, that everyone is judging. You will quickly find every passing glance a malicious stare, every sound of innocent laughter directed mockingly towards you and every unintentional nudge and deliberate budge. Then reverse your expectation and imagine that everyone wants to be around you, or have heard great things about you. You will notice a big different, both in what you perceive and also how you react to it.

PROTECTION

Practice 4 - If you Can't Sweep it - Shake it Off

Broomsticks are age-old tools used to protect the house and ward off negativity - a simple practice you can use without having to bring in a broomstick to the office is to shake it off.

Step 1: Find a quiet space where you are happy to look a little silly!

Step 2: Physically shake your body as if you were shaking of water after a shower having forgotten your towel. (if it helps imagine a dog who has just got out of the sea!) Feel all of the negativity literally fly off your body like droplets of water.

This is specifically useful after any situation where you have had to use protection find time to shake it off and rebalance your energy.

WHAT DOES PROTECTION FEEL LIKE FOR YOU?

Use Biographical Visualisation to reconnect with a past memory and manifest the sensations again within your present. By doing this you are reaffirming your ability to feel them and reinforcing the pathways to receive them again.

PROTECTION

Your Toolkit

Top Essential Oils to Help with Protection

Calendula - there are many types of Calendula - the most common, which you will recognise is the marigold. Just like the beautiful orange flower itself, this oil will help with dispelling negative energy

Lavender - you will have potentially already tried this on your pillow to help sleep. It is wonderfully calming and also the oil that was said to have been the driver for an early 20th century French chemist, René-Maurice Gattefossé - to delve into what he called "Aromatherapie" after using Lavender oil to help heal a serious burn

Rose - a smell many will be familiar with, this essential oil is calming and restorative, also helping alleviate what weighs upon your mind

Top Crystals

Black Tourmaline – draws in negative energy, transforms it and releases the positive

Onyx – will develop your emotional and physical strength to increase your stamina during challenging situations

Obsidian – quiets an overactive mind

Smokey Quartz – helps clear out any old negative patterns that could be holding you back and empower clarity of mind

Listen

You brain has five different types of waves - Delta, Theta, Alpha, Beta and Gamma. Each corresponding to a different state from complete relaxation (Delta) through to peak performance (Gamma). The lower the frequency the more relaxation, the higher the frequency the more alert.

Binaural beats, quite literally meaning 'two ears', is when a tone with a slightly different frequency is played in each ear. They are received separately by the area of the brain that gathers auditatory input making your brain attempt to sync them - assisting in impacting your brain state.

Colour

Black - think of how enveloped we feel on a moonless night, how that darkness hides us in the shadows - wearing the colour black emulates this feeling of being able to hide or protect ourselves from negativity.

Although technically not a colour - black is quite literally black because it absorbs all the colours of the visible spectrum reflecting none back to be perceived by the eye. And just as it absorbs colour, it is excellent at absorbing negativity.

Touch

Both Plato and Aristotle wrote on the art of reading palms. Whilst they may be the 'lines upon which we think' they also provide points for healing, in this case, a rerduction of stress. Spread you hand out and using your thumb and index finger, massage the webbing between the thumb and index finger of your other hand for a few seconds.

Note - this point can induce labour, so it is advisable not to do if you are pregnant.

PROTECTION

Your notes:

Your notes:

PROTECTION

Peace of Mind & Balance

WHEN YOU MAKE PEACE WITH YOURSELF, YOU MAKE PEACE WITH THE WORLD

Maha Ghosananda

PEACE OF MIND AND BALANCE

Ironically, this is one of the intentions we battle most for, but if you chase something, the more it will keep running. This is especially true of peace of mind and balance - which can only be found upon being still and in reflection.

In life, we often live between running at 100% and exhaustion, happiness and stress, efficiency and lethargy. The higher the pendulum swings one way, the further it will swing the other way as momentum carries it.

You will find that the most lively, sparky people you meet - will also be the ones who need the most stillness and solitude to balance out their energy expenditure.

Difficulties arise we when we are not able to control the momentum of the pendulum to let it settle back to stillness, or when we become quite literally addicted to those highs and lows.

Practice 1: As Internal so External

When we think about peace of mind, we often thing purely from the place of the mind, but the mind works in symbiosis with the body. If your mind is running at 100% (probably trying to reach 120!) but you're stuck behind a desk this creates an internal in-balance. You know that feeling when you get home, and you are mentally exhausted but irritable?

To create balance you need to work your body as hard as you work your mind. Whatever flicks your switch – whether it is tennis, surfing, running, paddle boarding, walking or a good old gym session.

Give your body a chance to rebalance with your mind you when your head hits that pillow, it will be a good nights sleep.

Practice 2: Quieten the Internal Chatter

Our minds run at a phenomenal rate and we are fully conscious of it - from the moment we wake until our heads it the pillow. Whether your mind is reflecting on the past or projecting into the future - it is rarely peacefully oscillating in the here and now.

This exercise will help you bring peace into the present even if it is just for a few minutes a day.

Step 1: Find somewhere comfortable – either cross-legged on a mat or on a seat with your feet flat on the floor.

Step 2: Focus your eyes 2 – 3 meters in front of your body and keep them open.

Step 3: Draw your focus onto your breath and the rise and fall of your chest.

Step 4: Catch when your internal chatter starts up and when thoughts come into your mind (and they will) acknowledge them then allow them to pass

It's important to accept the thoughts as they arise then release them. Thoughts are as part of your mindscape as clouds are to the sky. Trying to block them is going to be like asking your mind not to think about pink elephants … yes like the one you just imagined! You get the gist.

Gradually increase your practice from 1 to 2 minutes upwards. And remember 60 seconds is better than nothing – be gentle and give yourself time to flex the quiet mind muscle.

Practice 3: Connect with Your Intuition

Another way of grounding yourself is to firmly plant your mind in the present. An easy way to do this is by connecting with the one skill that can only be accessed if you are truly in the here and now - your intuition.

Divination tools like pendulums, tarot or runes are a fantastic way of accessing your intuition. Below is a simple Tarot drawing practice that can be done daily:

Step 1: Pick up your Tarot pack

Step 2: Shuffle them whilst keeping your mind focused on your question such as "what guidance do I need for today"

Step 3: Break the pack in two – keeping them both back up, place then in-front of you in two piles

Step 4: Take the top card from the left side and turn it over – spend some time with the card to interpret its meaning for you. If it feels right place it somewhere prominent where you can refer back to its energy during the day

This exercise can be adapted for runes and also pendulums – whichever tool you are more drawn to work with.

If you haven't worked with these yet, head over to the Divination chapter in Need to Know. We touch on all three of these tools and how to use them.

PEACE OF MIND & BALANCE

Practice 4: From 101 to 3

You know that feeling of being so focused on something that you don't have space for anything else in your mind? By harnessing this in the form of active meditation, you can give your mind some well-needed peace and quiet by being totally focused on an activity outside of your head.

Ready to go from juggling 101 things to three?

Step 1: Find three round objects - lemons, oranges, eggs - whatever you have on hand.

Step 2: Hold one of the lemons in your dominant hand and put the other hand behind your back. Practice throwing and catching the lemon. Get used to feeling the weight, how much force you require to throw it up to a certain height.

Step 3: Repeat with the other hand

Step 4: Put both hands out, lemons in palms and throw the one in your dominant hand up in the air, as it begins to drop, throw the other lemon up - aim to catch them in the same hand they came from

Step 5: Repeat but this time aim to catch them in the opposite hands

After you have finished take note on how your mind feels. Chances are it will feel a lot clearer! This is a great practice to use if your trying to solve a complex task. The break will give your mind a rest and allow your subconscious to keep whirring away on the problem unencumbered.

WHERE DO YOU FEEL MOST AT PEACE?

Use Biographical Visualisation to reconnect with a past memory and manifest the sensations again within your present. By doing this you are reaffirming your ability to feel them and reinforcing the pathways to receive them again.

**PEACE OF MIND
& BALANCE**

Your Toolkit

Top Essential Oils to Help with Peace of Mind and Balance

Patchouli - strongly grounding and centring. Its concentration of sesquiterpenes helps to relax the emotional centre of the brain. If you don't actually like the smell mix it with lavender or citrus to make it slightly more enjoyable!

Neroli - it's used in ancient Egypt to support the healing of mind, body, and spirit. This oil will help to balance emotions and promote peace.

Crystal clarity

Crystals can be worn, carried or even incorporated into everyday items such as pens, water bottles, mugs even draw handles. If you can imagine it - you will probably we able to find it!

Petrified wood will gently ease you back into your centre to find balance and stillness

Snowflake Obsidan assists in balancing your yin and yang energies

Rose Quartz promotes inner peace

Lepidolite quite literally from the Greek meaning scale this crystal helps restore balance and harmony

Colour

Unsurprisingly nature is full of balancing colours - if you can get outside - go watch the leaves on a tree or the clouds moving in the sky. If you can't get out of the office, try finding a window in the office, grab a coffee and watch from there.

If all else fails, or you stuck in the office on an all-nighter, then get creative with your screensaver - images of the ocean and sky might even be more inspiring than those from your office window!

Sound

Pop onto YouTube and search for a track at 528 Hz. Also known as the DNA repair frequency, it's the frequency the sun resonates at, as well as colour green (528nm).

Close your eyes and listen through headphones for optimal impact.

PEACE OF MIND & BALANCE

Your notes:

Your notes:

**PEACE OF MIND
& BALANCE**

>

LISTEN WITH INTENT DO NOT LISTEN TO REPLY

Improve Communication

IMPROVE COMMUNICATION

Communication is multifaceted and complex, from the more obvious use of language -spoken or written, through to tone of voice, gestures and body positioning.

Human communication ironically often leads to confusion. Although language enables us to get across complex ideas and concepts, there is a lot of room for miscommunication.

On a basic level, language is effectively the mode to translate or encode what is going on in our minds. When we communicate, even with ourselves, we automatically search for the best words we can find that can express the feeling, emotion or need.

However, the words we use are the ones we have we learnt and signified throughout our life, based on our own personal experiences. When an interlocker receives these words, they then need to reverse the process – translating or decoding the words we use, calling upon their signification of those words based on their own personal experience.

Now add in that we don't always say what we think or indeed think what we say and how we can use language to hide our own personal insecurities - there's a lot of room for crossed wires.

When we don't speak what we think there is a discord between our inner world and outer voice, which is felt by those around us - they may not be able to put their finger on it, but they will sense it.

Although what we communicate can needs be constrained at times by both situation and interlocutor, especially within a corporate environment, there are ways we can speak intentionally and from the heart.

Practice 1: Get clear on the outcome

If you don't really understand what you are saying – no one else will.

Step 1: Sit somewhere quiet and start with what you want the outcome of your communication to be – how do you want your words to be received?

Step 2: Imagine you are saying this too
- yourself
- a child
- a grandparent
- a friend

Step 3: How would they react? Are you clear enough? Would the outcome be what you envisaged?

Practice 2: Learn how to Listen

Communication is not just about speaking; it's about listening too. Unfortunately, so often nowadays we listen to reply – formulating our responses whilst someone is still speaking.

Start to purely listen when others speak - fully engaging in the speaker. This means not only stemming your inner voice but also removing all the ways you would usually 'respond' including positive reinforcements such as 'yes' or nodding your head. Focus solely on them and their words - your response will reinforce or negate if required after that person has spoken.

Step 1: Find a friend, colleague, significant other

Step 2: Take it in turns to talk for 60seconds (building up to 3minuites) about something

Step 3: Whoever isn't speaking must listen in absolute silence and focus purely on listening – no nodding, 'ummm'ing or the like – just listen

Step 4: Reverse roles

Step 5: Tell each other what you heard

Once you get over the discomfort, you will soon find the pace of your other conversations begin to slow down – both ways, and understanding improve. The person speaking will not feel they need to rush to fit in what they have to say, and likewise, the listener will know that they have a chance to speak so will stop interrupting as much. and likewise, the listener will know that they have a chance to speak so wilstop interrupting as much.

You will discover you can hear better and talk slower, just by being an active liistener. In problem resolution, allowing someone to speak without interruption will often guide them to find their own resolution.

Practice 3 – Its Never Stupid to Ask

So often in business, we may be afraid to say we don't know. You have no idea how many CXOs are unfamiliar with terminology fundamental to grasping a concept - especially technical. 90% won't stop you in front of the group to ask for clarification, they will wait until after the talk and come up to you in private.

Step 1: Be present in every conversation and if there is something you don't understand – make a point to ask for clarification every time. Everyone knows something someone else doesn't - if we all knew everything that everyone else did - then there would be little point for conversation! This also shows you are active in the discourse and gives others the opportunity to feel like they are adding value.

Step 2: When you speak always pause at points and ask if what you are saying is clear. Just because you think it makes sense doesn't mean everyone else does.

Step 3: Be patient with others when they ask for clarification over something you havesaid - create the kind of space you would like others to make for you.

IMPROVE COMMUNICATION

Practice 4: Learn how to communicate silently

Get back to the basics and start talking (and listening) to those who don't communicate with language. There has been a lot of literature and studies in recent years about how trees communicate. Although they don't have mouths and you don't have roots – that doesn't make communication impossible.

Step 1: Go outside for a walk and wander around greeting everything you see - the trees, flowers, birds.

Step 2: If If you feel particularly drawn to a certain tree or flower, then keeping a respectable distance, ask if you are okay to come closer. Depending on the esponse either continue with Step 2 or move to Step 3.

Step 3: Ask a question - and listen to the response. As in the chapter on Self Knowledge - the response may come in images, feeling, sensation or colour - keep your mind open and gently allow the impressions to rest upon you then take note.

Step 4: When you are finished say thank you and gently move away.

WHEN WAS THE LAST TIME YOU HAD A REALLY GOOD CONVERSATION?

Use Biographical Visualisation to reconnect with a past memory and manifest the sensations again within your present. By doing this you are reaffirming your ability to feel them and reinforcing the pathways to receive them again.

IMPROVE COMMUNICATION

Your Toolkit

Top Essential Oils for Improving Communication

Focus on incense and essential oils that will help your open up your throat chakra.

Frankincense is often used in meditation to aid in spiritual practice it aids in mental and emotional grounding. Used in ancient rituals for aiding in communion with gods.

Tangerine similar aroma to orange this oil is excellent in uplifting the spirit and bringing about a sense of security

Top Crystals

Carnelian – will help boost confidence to find your voice

Amazonite – connecting the chakras in the throat, heart, and solar plexus will help intuition and the ability to communicate with strength and compassion.

Chrysocolla - aids in releasing negative beliefs and strengthening motivation. Fantastic for public speakers and communicating to large audiences

Sound

Silence can be golden! Turn off all distractions and focusing solely on the person speaking. They will feel your undivided attention and react in kind.

Colour

When communicating, linking colour to what you are talking about will reinforce your verbal messaging.

- Presenting to a team or group about a new idea - think greens
- Big structural changes that might cause concern use blues
- Need to get people motivated - go bright hues
- Want to drive a message home about risks - good old red will never fail

Whether you are messaging using multiple colours to support various messages or just one, there are many ways to incorporate them into your communication. From well-placed objects in your background during a video call to clothing or in presentations themselves if using slides.

Touch

Try not to fold your arms, stick your hands in pockets or clasp your palms together.

When you speak keep your arms (naturally!) in-front of you and your palms gently open. This non verbal signal shows willingness to open up and will also encourage others to do the same driving improved communication

IMPROVE COMMUNICATION

Your notes:

Your notes:

IMPROVE COMMUNICATION

> I don't seek to understand everything, but if it crosses my path - I hope to at least be able to identify it

NEED TO KNOW

SECTION TWO

Grounding

Grounding is a little like tying a red thread to the entrance of the minotaur's cave so that no matter how far you go, you know you can trace your way back.

Throughout the day, we can be faced with a vast number of scenarios, all of which require not only energy from us, but also require us to receive energy from others.

Ever had a day where you finish and just feel worried, a bit out of sorts, off-kilter or downright high? That's your energy reacting ... when it goes too high, or too low – it's not balanced, and it's going to tire you out.

Top 5 ways to ground yourself:

1. Wear red socks

2. Rub sesame oil on the bottom of your feet and the lobes of your ears

3. Set your alarm 10-30 minutes early and give yourself time to wake up your body slowly from sleep

4. Get the largest organ of your body grounded
    - Let the palms of your hands rub your arms, torso and legs and be present in the tingling feeling in your palms and on your skin.

5. Before you're about to go into a situation that requires focus, achieving an objective or might involve a difficult conversation

Sit down with your feet flat on the floor - breathe in an out once:

- Engage your ears What can you hear? What can you hear beyond those sounds?
- Engage your nose. What can you smell? What can you smell beyond that?
- Engage your eyes. What can you see? What can you see beyond them?
- Engage your body. What can you feel against your skin? What can you feel beyond this?
- Engage your taste. What can you taste? What can you taste beyond that?

Stand up straight and imagine roots growing out of the soles of your feet, through your shoes and down. Stay with them as they bury through the concrete and foundations of the building, then hit the cool, moist soil and work their way deeper and deeper into the earth.

When you feel they are deep enough pause for a moment there and draw your consciousness up and back to your heart.

GROUNDING

Crystals

We identified specific crystals for each of the 7 personal drivers of Corporate Challenges, their properties each aiding in the individual areas. Find more about how to choose your crystals, why you need to cleanse them and how you can make the most out of these beautiful bones of the earth.

Choosing your crystals
Every crystal has certain qualities that each individual will interact with differently. So whilst one person may find a crystal incredibly relaxing - another may not. When you choose your crystals always go with your intuition. If it feels good, use it. If not, find an alternative.

Different ways You can use Crystals
We only have so many fingers for rings and our pockets are only deep enough for so many tumble-stones! You can below a few other ideas on using Crystals in the Workplace:

- On your desk:
    - Coasters
    - Tea Strainers
    - Crystal feature Pieces

- To keep on/with you
    - Rings
    - Tumble Stones
    - Necklaces
    - Bracelet

Cleansing your crystals
Wherever you go, you exchange energy with the world around you – objects, people, nature. This energy leaves an imprint which can be felt by others. Have you ever walked into a room just after an argument? Or sat in a space that is used for prayer or healing? Objects also hold the energy of those they have been in possession of so it's important whenever you purchase a new crystal or piece of jewellery you cleanse it of all past energy and do this regularly – to also cleanse them of your energy.

Simple cleansing techniques:
- Hold your crystal under the tap and request that all previous energies be cleanses and released
- Place your Crystals under the light of a full-moon

Get to know them
As with everything what we put in, we get out. Spend time with your crystals, treat them with respect and get to know their energy. You can simply start out by holding one, closing your eyes and focusing on the feelings and sensations that come to you. Note the differences between how each of them makes you feel.

A great exercise is to lay your crystals out ono a table, close your eyes and mix them around ensuring there is enough space between them and so you can't clearly identify which crystal is where. Using your preferred hand, place your palm a few inches above them and move it – paying attention to the different energies you feel. You will get to the point where you can identify which crystal is under your hand just based on the energy it gives off!

CRYSTALS

IN XANADU DID KUBLA KHANA STATELY PLEASURE-DOME DECREE:WHERE ALPH, THE SACRED RIVER, RAN THROUGH CAVERNS MEASURELESS TO MAN

Coleridge

Divination Tools

Our subconscious holds an infinite amount of knowledge that our conscious mind cannot process, blocks or just ignores. Divination tools are a fantastic way of accessing this innate knowledge. We touched on the tarot in one of the practices. Below are a full list of divination tools and how they can be used.

Have some fun with them and try a few out - you may find an unexpected skill with. Runes, candles or coffee reading!

Types of Divination Tools:

- **Pendulum** - using a suspended weight usually for yes/no answers
- **Palmistry** - reading the lines and patterns on a palm
- **Cartomancy** - using cards such as Tarot or Oracle
- **Scrying** - gazing into a surface such as a mirror, still water or crystal ball
- **Pyromancy** - gazing into fire
- **Osteomancy** - reading bones
- **Runes** - reading symbols carved into throwing stones or wood pieces
- **Tasseomancy** - reading tea leaves or coffee granules

Three of the most accessible and arguably useful for business as well as life are Pendulums, Cartomancy and Runes.

Cartomancy

There are hundreds of different card decks you could choose from the more traditional Rider Waite through to horse, oracle and angel cards – even a pack of playing cards can be used.

Similar to crystals, go for the ones that you feel the greatest affinity with and spend some time getting to know them. When you do draw them, don't rush immediately for the accompanying guide to translate them. It is very worthwhile to sit with the card or cards and feel what they are telling you using the images printed on them to guide you. This way you will become adept at reading them far quicker and also be giving your intuition a chance to show you what it can do.

Shuffling your cards
Shuffle your cards while you ask your question, it will help direct your intention.

Choosing your Cards and a Simple Spread
After you have shuffled them, the simplest way to choose them is to split them into three piles - from the left past, present and future. Take the top card from each pile and use these in your reading.

What is a spread?
Simply put a spread is how many cards and the way you lay them. There are a huge number of spreads available from single cards through to multiple as you get more adventurous.

Caring for your Cards
Everything you touch leaves an energetic imprint and your cards are no exception. To cleanse your pack after a reading, simply shuffle them with the intention of clearing the residual energy. If you. feel you need something more, pass them through the smoke of a sage incense stick.

Pendulums

Choose a pendulum in the same way you choose your crystal – go with what feels right. Like with tarot decks there are a multitude to choose from and sometimes they choose you - if you are able to get to a crystal shop in person, watch for the ones that begin to spin in your presence. Remember, above all, a pendulum is a conduit. Something as simple as a needle on a thread or ring on a piece of string will bring as accurate answers as the most elaborate ones out there.

Pendulums need no interpretation – they will give you a clear answer (provided you ask a straightforward question). If you choose this as your preferred divination technique remember to cleanse your pendulum as you would a crystal. Then you will need to learn which way is its 'yes' and which way its 'no', in other words to programme it.

Programming a Pendulum

Hold your pendulum up and ask a clear question you know the answer to like "Do I live in London?" or "Is my birthday the 21st June 1985?" watch which way it circles – this will be your "yes" direction. As with all methods of divination find your space and focus on your breathing for a few minutes before using them – if your mind is in chaos or elsewhere, you will find you either don't get a response, or it is incorrect.

Holding a pendulum

Ideally, sit straight up with both feet flat on the floor, hold the
string, top bead or fob or your pendulum between your thumb and forefinger, steady your elbow on a flat surface and arch your wrist slightly

Cleansing your Pendulum

Before you start using your pendulum it is important, as with all your other tools, that you cleanse it of previous energies. You can do this by placing it under running water, leaving it overnight under a full moon or letting it swing in Sage or Palo Santo incense.

Runes

A little more complex but very rewarding you can use runes in a similar way to tarot – they will hint at answers, but you need to interpret them. The engravings on runes can be from various alphabets, the oldest being the Elder Futhark.

Runes can be made from pebbles, pieces of wood, bone or stone – again whatever you feel works best for you is right for you.

When using runes, like with all divination tools, spend time getting to know then, to understand the meanings behind the symbols as well as the material they are carved upon.

Your Runes will attune to your energy by keeping them in a pocket or bag close to you. Two simple ways to cleanse them are to leave them outside for 24 hours or smudge them with sage.

As with every divination technique the better the question the better the answer

I DO WISH YOU WOULD COME TO YOUR SENSES

Everyone

Your Senses

Quite literally, our senses send information to help the brain perceive and understand the world around us, they are the means through which we can react and interact in the present.

The senses don't have to just react; they can also be harnessed and intentionally primed to help us. Most of the tools in the Toolkits involve using the senses with this goal in mind.

Aristotle devoted a chapter to each of what he felt were our main senses in De Anima. Since then, the idea of 'five senses' has become ingrained within our education. But there are many more – between 21 to 53 depending upon who you ask - from Thermoception and Mechanoreception through to Proprioception. The latter, the ability to keep track of where our body parts are in space is the official 'sixth sense'!

Awareness is key to our experience - so let's bring some attention to what we already know about our traditional five - then if your curiosity has been wetted, there are a multitude of others you can explore at your pace.

Hearing

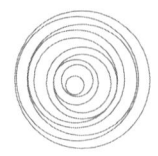

From listening to music you love through to singing along, dancing, meditating and playing an instrument. There are a multitude of ways you can use those vibrations picked up by your ears.

Ways to use Sound

- Vibrations produced by sound waves can be physically applied via tuning fork therapy
- Immerse yourself within sound waves during gong sessions
- Binaural beats
    - quite literally meaning 'two ears', is when a tone with a slightly different frequency is played in each ear to help your brain enter certain states. The lower the frequency the more relaxation, the higher the frequency the more alert.
- Turned up with the windows down while driving on a sunny day!

If you have ever wanted to actually see sound waves and the impact they have upon the water (worth keeping in mind the human body is 70% water) – check out Masaru Emoto's experiments. Truly mind-blowing.

Sight

Light has been use was used by Egyptians, Greeks, Romans and other major cultures. The Egyptians would work to restore imbalance by means of applying colour to the body, or in colour halls where sunlight was shone through coloured gems onto those seeking healing.

Colour is effectively radiation of varying wavelengths which are perceived by the eye then sent to the brain to process. Colours with the greatest wave lengths require far more energy to be perceived, therefore they stimulated the brain. Whilst colours with shorter wavelengths require less energy and as such have a calming effect.

This is why colours such as red, orange and yellow are used to stimulate the surroundings and surrounding people, whilst blues, greens and lighter colours are used to aid relaxation.

Taste

Our brain and body function based on the food ingested, metabolised and reallocated within us. Quite literally, we are what we eat, not only for the nutrients we can absorb but also how the gut-brain axis ties our digestive system to how we feel. If your gut is happy ... chances are you will be too.

A great example of how our senses work together is to see how touch and colour can impact how we perceive what it is we taste.

Touch

This is the one sense that can both be given and received. Whether presented in the form of energy that can activate healing such as Reiki, laying of hands, acupressure, and massage or what touches us such as crystals.

Stemming back to the ancient Sumerians of Mesopotamia, Crystals were placed on specific points on the body to induce energy flow and / or healing. This connects to another field of knowledge - the idea of our Chakras. These are specific centres of energy running through our body, each responsible for a different area of our physical and spiritual health and development.

The ideas of where we touch being as important as what we use is highlighted in practices such as reflexology and acupuncture among others.

Smell

So two facts I am pretty sure you didn't know:
- The average person can detect over one trillion different scents
- Your own personal odour is as individual as your fingerprint

Smells send messages from the nose into the nervous system to the part of the brain that controls emotions. So, while we can be pleasantly surprised by a scent that brings back a fond childhood memory, we can also influence our emotions and actual physiology through actively exposing ourselves to scents with a deliberate intention.

Just remember that smell can be extremely personal - the perfume of cookies baking in an oven may bring back fond memories of cooking with your grandma or terrifying ones of the time you burnt the half of the kitchen down!

Aromatherapy

Aromatherapy has been used in ancient India, China and Egypt through to Hippocrates (460-377BC) and into the modern world. We have highlighted different essential oils to use the toolkits which will aid with the 7 personal drivers of Corporate Challenges.

Essential oils are very different from perfume, they are far stronger and need to be used diluted. Here are a few ways to use them:
- diluted in a carrier oil such as sweet almond oil or apricot kernel oil and massaged into the skin or specific points such as the pulse.
- a few drops on a scarf or item of clothing (be careful of staining)
- add a few drops to water and use in a diffuser
- sprinkle a few drops in a bath

Essential Oils all have their own individual properties and although we have given you an overview in the Toolkits, they are well worth looking into if have the time.

Your Sixth Sense

Officially our sixth sense is proprioception, it allows us to keep track of where our body parts are in space.

But more commonly the term 'sixth sense' is considered the ability to know things that aren't fully understandable from the information presented to us logically.

You know that feeling when you go into a meeting that something is going to happen, or when your interviewing a candidate and you get that feeling they are just right. You will find this often referred to as gut instinct.

We have been taught that logical processing leads to infallible decision making to the point that even if something 'doesn't feel right', we are more likely to go against our feelings and align with logic. It has been drilled into us that intuition is whimsical, subjective and unreliable.

But that 'gut feeling' is also processed in the brain, the information it is based on just happens outside of your consciousness so you may not be aware of what has created it. That doesn't mean it isn't valuable or potentially accurate.

The brain is, in reality, one great a predictive machine, automatically filtering out what it believes as irrelevant information and using past experiences to enforce our decision making. You will all have probably seen the video of people playing basketball and you will all have also probably had to watch it a second time to 'find' the man dressed as a giant gorilla walking through the middle of them. You didn't expect to see something in a certain context - so you didn't.

So listen, open your mind up to other possibilities even those unexpected and you will begin to see a lot more than you expect. With time and practice you can learn to work on your intuition, and the more you do, the more you will learn to trust that 'sixth sense'.

> *THE MOON IS A LOYAL COMPANION. IT NEVER LEAVES. IT'S ALWAYS THERE, WATCHING, STEADFAST, KNOWING US IN OUR LIGHT AND DARK MOMENTS, CHANGING FOREVER JUST AS WE DO.*
>
> *EVERY DAY IT'S A DIFFERENT VERSION OF ITSELF. SOMETIMES WEAK AND WAN, SOMETIMES STRONG AND FULL OF LIGHT. THE MOON UNDERSTANDS WHAT IT MEANS TO BE HUMAN. UNCERTAIN. ALONE. CRATERED BY IMPERFECTIONS*

Tahereh Mafi

Listen to the Rhythms

Our bodies are moved by a multitude of rhythms – from both the business world and the natural one. From official office hours, quarterly reviews and fiscals through to circadian rhythms, seasons and moon cycles.

While some rhythms we can choose to allow into our lives – others we have no choice over. Work rhythms can necessarily be changed – for example, moving from a career in sales to a career in engineering enables you to step outside of sales cycles and into development cycles. Other rhythms are set by nature, and their pull and release have been built into the very fabric of our being, more often than not without question.

Take for example your circadian and infradian rhythms – those physical, mental and behavioural changes that occur either response to the daily cycles of light and darkness or cycles of longer periods like those impacting periods in women or hibernation in bears.

Being in rhythm with the cycles in the world around us is crucial – harmony is created when the external and the internal work together. So listening specifically for those rhythms and allowing ourselves to tune in with them is invaluable to deepening the work we do both inside and outside of the office.

So let's take a look at a few rhythms ...

The Moon

Astrologically the moon moves from a new moon waxing to the slim crescent shape to the first quarter then into the ripe gibbous moon before it becomes fully visible as a full moon. It then begins its journey waning back through gibbous to quarter then to crescent before it begins a new cycle.

It is common knowledge that the tides are impacted by the moon. Some winemakers will harvest their grapes and gardeners plant their seeds according to the lunar cycle. Women can find that their menstruation or ovulation aligns to a particular phase.

Some of us can be more sensitive at specific points in the lunar cycle and probably less likely, but legend has it, that some even develop a concerning hairy aspect and start growling!

So how can you work with moon cycles?

Understanding the Different Moon Phases & How to Work with their Energy

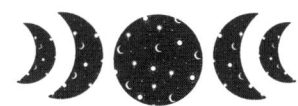

For a moment, think about the ebb and flow of the sea's tides – while they are flowing, there is progressive, expansive energy – upwards and forwards. While they are ebbing, they are withdrawing and removing themselves quite literally from the shores. We can see the same rhythm in the moon from where we stand on earth.

The ebb and flow of nature reminds us of the importance of balance. We can not always be starting new projects, striving forward with eyes on the horizon. We need to also have moments to pause, the reflect upon what is working and what isn't for us and give our selves a pat on the back before we continue, leaving behind what no longer serves us.

You can align this momentum with the movement of the moon:

First Quarter (Waxing Moon)
When the energy around us is expanding and increasing during a waxing moon, it is an excellent opportunity for us to initiate our own projects, start new things or create new beginnings.

Full Moon
Fulfilment of a cycle – time for reviewing what you have achieved and giving thanks, releasing what is not needed, recognising what is ending. Recharge your tools under the light of a full moon.

Last Quarter (Waning Moon)
The energy of the waning moon is great to piggyback to release what no longer serves you from negative emotions through to bad habits or toxic situations to start afresh in the new moon

New Moon
A blank canvas focus your attention on the space and what you want to invite into your life to start building or creating upon it

'ANYONE CAN BE A MILLIONAIRE, BUT TO BECOME A BILLIONAIRE YOU NEED AN ASTROLOGER."

J P Morgan

The Planets

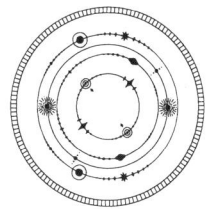

The planets, and their positions throughout the year as they come in and out of view from earth, are believed to influence life based on qualities attributed to them. These attributes are well over 2000 years old.

We are all impacted to varying degrees by the planets' movements also based upon when we were born. Each planet rules over a different part of our psyche depending on where it was upon our birth – symbolising a universal component of our experience here on earth. With your birth date, time and place you can build a chart giving not only get a pretty accurate reading on your personality but also what has been and will be coming for you by mapping where planets will be on your chart and their influences over the coming months/years.

Below is a very basic overview of the Planets and what parts of our psyche they rule over (in astrology - the sun, moon and Pluto are counted as luminary bodies)

- **The Sun -** Personality, consciousness, the basic self (the ego), vitality and stamina

- **The Moon -** feelings, emotions, instinctive drives and overall moods. Strongly connected to the subconscious

- **Mercury -** Reason covering thought structure how information is absorbed and how we communicate

- **Venus -** Pleasure, beauty and sociability

- **Mars -** Aggression, sense of competition, sex, action, desire, passion, courage

- ♃ **Jupiter** - Growth, optimism, abundance, understanding, luck

- ♄ **Saturn** - Responsibility, obligation, ambition, structure, law, restriction, discipline

- ♅ **Uranus** - Unpredictable changes, reformation, rebellion, eccentricity

- ♆ **Neptune** - Intuition, Mysticism, Imagination, Dreams

- ♇ **Pluto** - Evolution, rebirth, power, transformation

Retrogrades

You may already be familiar with the term Mercury retrograde – in recent years it has become increasingly popular especially on social media with phrases like "Mercury retrograde made me do it"; or "buckle up its Mercury retrograde."

A retrograde is quite literally when it looks like a planet is either still or moving backwards in the sky (it's actually not - it's just an optical illusion). Mercury is the planet of communication, so a Mercury retrograde is considered as 'reversing' or negatively impacting communication.

However, it's not just mercury that moves backwards – all the planets do.. And each time they go into retrograde – what they represent can be seen to move backwards.

Whether our destinies are written in the stars, or they are only a map that can be deviated from, it is an old art used to advise kings, warn of plagues, and predict futures.

The Seasons

One of the most prominent rhythms in nature that you will be most aware of is the changing of the seasons.

Officially, divisions in a year are marked by weather and the changing of daylight times. These were originally also the driver for what was big business for thousands of years - agriculture. Whilst Farmers still use Almacs as guides to plant and harvest, seasons are less tied to business but still intricately tied to you and your place within your part of the world.

Seasons still provide us with markers for the turning of a year. Moments that, like the rhythm of the moon, also carry their own energy. They are fantastic to use as markers to remind us to also balance our time. Just as it cannot always be spring, we cannot always live in a growth phase, our time here will flow like the seasons between sowing, growth, harvesting and reflection.

Winter - a time for introspection and laying plans for the future. A closing out of the past year and resolutions for the new year all belong here.

Spring - the period for new-birth, for the intentions we sowed during the cold introspection of the winter months to germminate and begin to burst forth from our minds.

Summer - when the world is buzzing with life, a time to remember to still tend for those goals and dreams in those warm months in the knowledge of a fruitful reward come harvest time.

Autumn - completion of a cycle; harvesting and collecting of all we have sown during the year. A time of celebration and basking in the warming in preparation for the coming season

Wherever you are in the world, take note of the seasons. You are not a separate entity from the world around you. You are intricately connected. Learning to flow with the energy around you will leave you feeling connected, aligned and in harmony with the world you live in.

It can be challenging to find new ways to approach the old system of work when our minds are taken up with to-dos, targets, bonuses and video-calls. Which is why Corporate Hippie came into being.

This book can be the only thing you read, or it could be the foundation to a library of knowledge - wherever you are in life, there is a myriad of tools you can use to exercise that inner hippie.

From the moment we are born, we never stop growing – physically, mentally, and spiritually. I hope this book has inspired you to grow in ways you hadn't imagined before entering between its covers because caught between work and home is this beautifully fragile moment of life – you, who deserves to be both wild and well-heeled.

About the Author

It took me a long time to find the balance between the business women and the hippie – they are both parts of me that I have explored in their multicoloured extremes over the years - never quite satisfied living as one without the other.

My young world was full of nature and magic, it planted the seeds of an innate curiosity about the world we are surrounded by and our experience within it. Many of my first memories are walking with my Grampa in the Herefordshire countryside. He taught my brothers and I what tracks belonged to which animals, how alongside a plant that could hurt you was often the plant that could provide the cure and ways to read the stars to understand where we were. Alongside this were the legends of my Nana's forays into the spirit world and Great Nana's tea leaf reading.

After trotting off to university to study Italian, English literature and Arabic, I found the same magic within the small winding cobbled streets of Bergamo. I would dash from lecture to lecture along the narrow streets of the old town, books overflowing with knowledge about ancient cultures and their languages, clutched to my chest.

These years came to a rather abrupt end when I started working within the rough and ready, bonus driven world of recruitment. However, I found a new side to myself in the 7am starts and cosmopolitan fuelled lunches - one that loved the adrenaline of the chase, the feeling of smashing targets, and the financial gains that resulted. Within three years, I was spent and decided to set off in search of what I had lost.

The last 10 years have been quite a journey - from training in the old ways with a shaman on the border of Wales to sitting in silence for days under the guidance of tutors on the Shambhala Path of the Warrior. I have found patterns within ancient knowledge such as how the same archetypes found in the Tarot are also relatable to those within Transpersonal psychotherapy and Astrology. And also how the way we view the world and our human preoccupations is not so different to those in ancient Babylon as I clumsily translated Akkadian texts into English.

Perhaps above all, since returning to a career in corporate, I have learn't that what used to feel like two very different worlds - are actually two sides of the same coin. Two sides of modern day human experience, that when brought together can be not only extremely rewarding, but balancing, joyful and soul filling.

★

Printed in Great Britain
by Amazon